37 Animal Heads Mandala in this book

THIS BOOK BELONGS TO

_____

_____

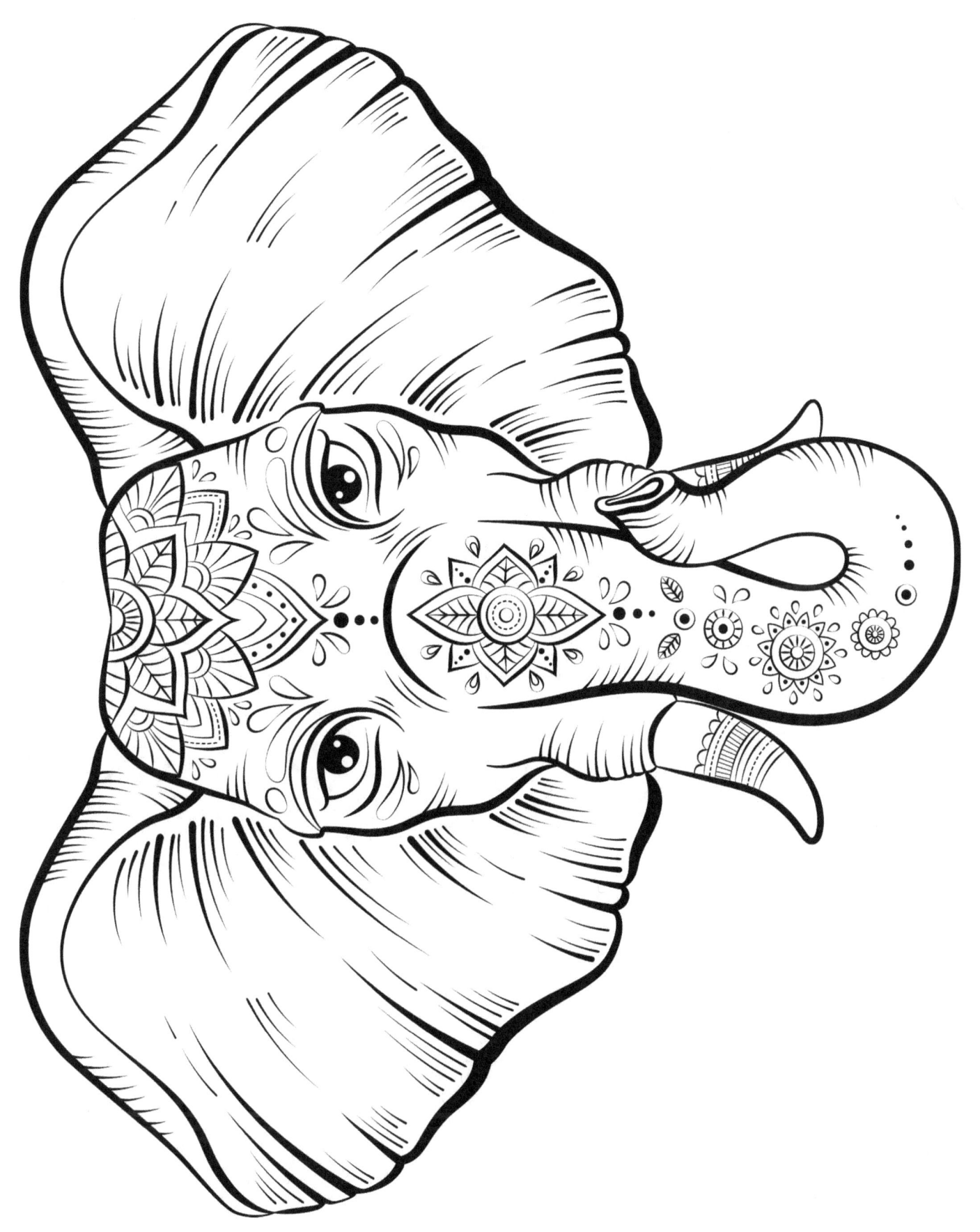

Example From Adult Coloring Book Vol.1

Animal Mandala Patterns

Example From Adult Coloring Book **Vol.2**

Animal Mandala Patterns

Example From Adult Coloring Book **Vol.3**

Animal Mandala Patterns

THANK YOU

www.ingramcontent.com/pod-product-compliance
Lightning Source LLC
Chambersburg PA
CBHW081410280526

45788CB00009B/3048